KEEPING A
COOL HEAD
IN A
HOT MARKET

Traders Press, Inc.®
PO Box 6206
Greenville, SC 29606

Serving Traders Since 1975
http://www.traderspress.com

Ruth Barrons Roosevelt

ISBN: 0-934380-99-6

This publication is designed to provide accurate and authoritative information with regard to the subject matter covered. It is sold with the understanding that the publisher is not engaged in rendering legal, accounting or other professional advice. If legal advice or other expert assistance is required, the services of a competent professional person should be sought.

Layout and Cover Design
Teresa Darty Alligood
Editor and Graphic Designer
Traders Press, Inc.®

Traders Press, Inc.®
PO Box 6206
Greenville, SC 29606
Serving Traders Since 1975
http://www.traderspress.com

PUBLISHER'S FOREWORD

Traders Press takes pride in publishing this material with what I think is one of the "coolest" titles ever assigned to a book dealing with trading. As a longtime trader myself (over 40 years and counting), I feel that the ability to keep a "cool head" while coping with the considerable stresses created when dealing in leveraged instruments and fast-moving "hot markets" is one of the prime requisites to success in trading.

This title (*Keeping a Cool Head in a Hot Market*) was originally one of a list of titles under consideration for another **Traders Press** publication, *Investor Skills Training: Managing Emotions and Risk in the Market* by Dr. Rob Ronin, another excellent publication which readers of this material will find to be of exceptional value and interest. I'm indebted to my good friend Rob for his kind permission to use this title, which is of his devising, for this book.

Equally in my debt is my friend Ruth Roosevelt, who graciously consented to write this book to "fit the title" as her starting point. A trading coach who has helped countless traders learn how to manage emotions, resolve conflicts, divorce ego, discover and change limiting beliefs, and execute a winning system with confidence, Ruth is herself a seasoned trader with many years of experience in various markets and in a multitude of market conditions, including the "hot markets" of which her writing so eloquently speaks in this book. Her services will prove of extraordinary value to traders who seek her counsel. Readers who find this book of interest will doubtless want to continue reading Ruth's other writings, which include *Exceptional Trading: The Mind Game, 12 Habitudes of Highly Successful Traders, and Overcoming 7 Deadly Sins of Trading.* These works should be considered indispensable additions to your trading library. Full details may be found at:
http://www.traderspress.org/detail.asp?product_id=1470

If you're the reader of a copy of the "E-book" version of this manuscript, you are encouraged to spend some time perusing the many features of our website at **http://www.traderspress.com** and to bookmark it for future reference and use. We have unusual and unique artwork and gifts for traders and investors, free weekly columns, trading book reviews, and many other features of vital interest to anyone with an interest in trading and the markets. We look forward to having you as a regular visitor.

Edward Dobson

Edward Dobson, President   January 1, 2005
Traders Press, Inc.
Greenville, SC
http://www.traderspress.com

The Sure Thing

Ruth Roosevelt

Our copious new riches all seemed so real,
as the market raced toward heaven
"Like a homesick angel"
(Someone had said).

Nasdaq: two thousand, three thousand,
four thousand, five
Once I made fifty thousand dollar
before I could take a bath.
Tech was the ticket as it marched and roared.

The rising tide cleansed all our mistakes.
We could do no wrong as the market
soared and soared.
Millionaires were born.
Heck, Billionaires too!

And then—just like that—it seemed,
It slid back down to earth.
Wine was turned into water.
Like fallen angels, we found
ourselves flat, face down
on the unyielding ground.

The Dilemma

At the core of trading—indeed investing as well—lies a crucial enigma. A trader must protect his capital: he must not lose his medium of investment. At the same time he must take advantage of the opportunities that come his way, but in so doing, he puts his capital at risk.

It's a balancing act. The trader must continually measure risk with reward and keep the two in a state of counterpoise. Truly, if nothing is ventured, nothing is gained. If you clutch the bird in the hand, you will not catch the two in the bush.   Too much hesitation in the face of movement, too much reluctance to enter a market, and the tide of fortune passes.

At the same time, rushing into a situation before it's mature leads to false signals and false hopes. In rushing the bush, you could lose the bird in the hand.

The trader's conundrum is to preserve the money she has while growing it at a rate commensurate with what the markets are offering.

Once the entry is commenced, the problem is just beginning. How long does she stay? How does she know when she's wrong? How does she know when the move has ended?

Grabbing small profits in a major move is a recipe for mediocrity at best and failure at worst. We've all heard the saying: "the money is made in the sitting." And, indeed, great fortunes have been made staying with a position through its ups and downs. The Warren Buffet's of this world have proven that.

On the other hand, we've all heard the stories of wealthy investors who die broke and broken hearted. Recently, I heard of a man who made $20,000,000. in the run up of the stock market going into March of 2000. Today he's lucky if he has $10,000. of it left.

We also know that those who make money trading take a lot of little losses and have a few large wins; while those who lose money trading take many small profits and have a few large losses. Yes, Jane and Johnny, you can go broke taking a profit. The general formula underlying trading success and failure can be simplified and summarized in a well known trading cliche: cut your losses and let your profits run. But traders don't seem able to do this.

Easier Said Than Done

Why do we do those things that work against us? And why do we do it again and again and again?

I was laughing with a weight loss client about my tendency to sell out my day trading positions early even though my research tells me it's generally best to wait until the close of the day's trading. He, a competitive bridge player, was completely puzzled by my behavior.

"Why would you do something that works against you?" he asked in a totally mystified tone.

"Why would you eat the carrot cake when you want to lose wait?" I countered.

He laughed and said, "I get it."

The Human Condition

Trading is no different than any other human behavior. Our personalities, our tendencies, our fears, our hopes all play themselves out in the trading arena. In spades.

Janice's Story

"It was early in 1980, and yet I still remember as if it were yesterday. Gold was on a tear. Each day it would ascend $10 or $15 or more. Of course, there were days it went down, but it was just part of the upward panorama. Each dollar gold moved equaled $100 per contract. Put together a few contracts, and you get the picture. We were on a ride to the moon."

"I was relatively new to trading, so I'd given $10,000 to my boyfriend to manage for me. Well, that's not exactly true. He'd given me the $10,000 and was managing it for me. My account was growing like wild mushrooms after a rain, and I was giving my compliments to the chef."

"Then one day he came home and told me he'd sold the gold. I was appalled. After all, gold was $800 an ounce and everybody knew it was going to $1000 an ounce. The Aden sisters had written that it was going to $4,000. I reacted in horror:

'You sold my _gold_?'

'Yes, I sold your gold. You're just like any other ungrateful client.'

"And then he just lost it, and started chasing me around the glass top table. Finally we both calmed down and I eased myself out of the apartment and into the elevator."

"In retrospect, he was right. While gold did get to $850, it never exceeded that and actually spent more than two decades basically selling off. Left to my own devices, I probably would have lost my shirt trying to buy every dip and never getting myself short."

Clean Perception

It's always obvious in retrospect, but in the heat of a hot market, we need experience and special skills and techniques to see clearly. Emotions cloud our vision. Ideas distort what we see. We tell ourselves stories. And we believe them.

Stories have power. True or false, they have hypnotic power. It could just be a simple quantitative story such as Janice's belief that gold was going to $1,000 an ounce and maybe even $4,000 an ounce. This became her legend. No doubt she unconsciously made pictures of the meaning of all this.

Stock brokers understand the power of story. They build a pitch about a stock that is designed to sell what they call the sizzle, the reason this stock has to go up.

"Where is the stock?" you ask.

"That's not the question to ask." they say. "Where is it going?"

"The technology is just coming to the forefront. The company's stock has not shot up yet. **You can still get in on the ground floor. But not for long!**"

Then they explain where the technology will be used and who will buy it. They build numbers of future profits and pictures of your own inevitable wealth. And sometimes they're right.

These narratives are strong, but not half as powerful as the tales we tell ourselves.

Kevin's Story

Kevin had a gift. He could tell when a big move was about to take place in a market. He'd caught many a move in crude oil both up and down.

And now he'd spotted another fortuity. This time it was in the grains. "This is going to be a big one." he told himself. Kevin was never one to simply watch a big opportunity from the side line. At the first sign of the move, he began to add long soybean contracts to his account. As it moved upward, he pyramided adding new contracts at higher prices. He knew his positioning was a little bit top heavy, but it was going his way, so he didn't worry about it. He was in a major bull move, and he was going to take full advantage of it.

Besides, he was convinced that with the drought in the Midwest, and basically across the country, there had to be a shortage of supply. It was too late in the season for any future rain to make a difference.

One Monday morning, as he was waiting for the market to open, he was anticipating the day's unfolding profits. The last few weeks had been so good to him. He was stunned when the market opened down. Instead of being up another $10,000, he was down $10,000!

He was incredulous. "What's going on?" he asked. "I don't believe this."

"Ah, it'll turn around." he answered himself. "It has to."

But it didn't. Not that day. Not that week. Not the next week. Nor the week after that. His profits dried up. At first Kevin made the decision not to act. He was so sure the market would turn back up that he didn't want to get out and be caught empty handed when it reversed.

Soon he went into loss, and soon thereafter the margin calls began. At this point he was no longer deciding. His indecision became a decision not to make a decision. In not deciding, he decided. He waited. He hesitated. Unsure, increasingly insecure, he was trapped by disinclination, debilitation, and the deterioration of his account. He was caught in the still turning place between decision and indecision.

At the same time, he stubbornly maintained his conviction that the fundamentals still favored a rising price in soybeans. He answered the margin calls, and continued losing. When he could no longer put up fresh money to answer the new calls, the firm sold out his position. Mercifully, somebody acted when he could no longer act.

Kevin's beliefs had been in conflict with the only true reality of market action which is price. It didn't really matter what Kevin believed or didn't believe. Price was against him, and his losses were real regardless of his opinions and expectations. An opinion doesn't mean anything unless it's backed up by price.

When we start to tell ourselves stories, we need to check it out against the market structure. Had Kevin prepared in advance, for an alternate occurrence, he would have recognized the adversity and been able to act in a timely way to save his profits.

There are some essential questions to ask before you put on a position:
- How much can I make?
- What is my risk?
- What will happen to tell me I'm wrong?
- Where will I know I'm no longer right?

Time, price, and volume are all valuable clues that can tell us when a marketmove is exhausted. But we need to pay attention them. We need to have some particular technical indicator, or set of conditions, that tells us what the trend is, when a trend is slowing down or reversing, and whether a market is trending or in congestion. Such an indicator or rule guideline can act as a reality check against any scenario trades we cook up.

We want to hold positive beliefs that support our trading, but these convictions are very different from the belief that a particular individual trade *has to be a winner.* Such a belief merely distorts our perception. And in a hot market, we have to keep our perceptions and interpretations clear and clean. We want to believe that through disciplined and effective trading we can and will make money, but *not necessarily that we'll make money in this one particular trade or market.*

Unconscious Conflicts

Sometimes distortions and misdeeds and non-deeds are based on unconscious assumptions and come from beyond what we are consciously seeing or telling ourselves. We need to have our conscious and unconscious minds in alignment with the positive value of creating wealth through trading. We may think we want to make money in a hot market, but some unstated conflicting notion causes us to sabotage our results.

Let's start with the important proposition of deserving wealth. Do you truly believe you deserve to be wealthy? Say to yourself, "**I deserve to be wealthy through my trading.**" Sit with it for a moment. What comes up for you?

Now try the simple "**I deserve.**" Do you wonder have you served enough to receive?

Add and say, "**I deserve to be.**" Many people as children were given the idea that they were unwanted or a mistake or that they're simply in the way or just not good enough.

This time stay with "**I deserve to be wealthy.**" Do you get thoughts that if you have wealth somebody else will have to do without? I know one trader who would get extremely uncomfortable when he was winning in a big way because he felt he was taking from others. Such ideas are based on a limited source world view and the concept that there isn't enough to go around. If there's only so much to go around, then they are not worthy of taking more than their share. Such a trader will find himself giving and re-giving back his profits.

Others get stuck on the idea of filthy lucre, that there's something dirty about money. Or they secretly believe that money is the root of all evil, or they feel that they must lay up treasure in heaven, but not on this earthly plain. Sometimes they view rich people as having made unsavory compromises to attain the money.

Some people have internalized family sayings and take them quite literally. We are poor, but we're happy. We are poor, but we love each other. We are poor, but we are honest. Unconsciously, they don't want to risk losing the happiness, the love, or the honesty. In their mind they have created a mutual exclusivity: if a person is rich, he won't be happy, or loved, or truthful.

Lastly say again, "**I deserve to be wealthy through my trading.**" What notions surface? Do you have the thought that trading is getting something for nothing? Do you get the feeling that you need to do a good hard day's work, or physical labor, or create a tangible product? Do you get the idea that trading is gambling and gambling is wrong? Is there any other reason why you think you might not deserve the fruits of your labors trading?

Some Beliefs that Support Successful Trading

- I'm in control of my own actions trading.
- I'm in control of myself and my future.
- I learn through my mistakes.
- I learn through my successes.
- My past failures have strengthened me.
- Each day I become a more seasoned, more effective trader.
- I get stronger and wiser every day by facing risk and adversity.
- There will be other major opportunities besides this one.
- The market provides me with oceans of opportunity.
- I know why I want to create wealth trading.
- There are no limits to the amount of money I can make.
- I use my money wisely for my own well being and the benefit of others.
- I can handle anything that comes up.
- I can solve any problem.
- Risk is essential to reward.
- I'm willing to give in order to receive.
- I always manage the risk.
- I accept the unknowability of the future.
- I prepare for surprise random events.
- I am committed to being an excellent trader.
- I know my rules, and I follow my rules.
- I value money because it has great power for good.
- Money comes to me easily.
- A part of all I make is mine to keep.
- I want to succeed as a trader.
- I deserve to succeed as a trader.
- I love trading. It is a privilege to trade.
- I am willing to work hard for what I believe in.
- I will do the necessary work and essential play to be a superior trader.

Make These Words Your Reality

An affirmation, such as the above statements, is a statement made in the present about the future as if it had already occurred in the past. Affirmations can be used to create and change belief systems.

Thought expands. What you think about becomes your reality. What is inside you, manifests outside yourself. If you don't like your circumstances, change the way you think. What is outside you, reflects inside and can be reevaluated and reinterpreted.

Focus on loss, you'll get loss. Focus on profits, and you'll find a way to create them.

How can you use affirmations to make them your reality? There are several ways.

One is to write them down and rewrite them ten times and do this twice a day.

Another way is to write down the affirmation and pause to let any objections come up. Then write the affirmation again and see what objections resurface. Keep doing this until there are no further objections.

You can also turn the affirmation into a question. The question keeps the objections away because we assume the truth of the question and go searching for the proof. "I deserve to succeed as a trader." becomes "In what ways do I deserve to succeed as a trader?" "I can handle anything that comes up." can be turned into "How can I handle anything that comes up?"

You can make the affirmation into an incantation. Chant it out loud and put energy behind it. Keep doing this until it begins to manifest in your life.

To make each affirmation more powerful make a visualization of it as true in your life. You can either make this a movie or a still picture or both. When you say the affirmation, see the image or visual stream.

You can mentally rehearse enacting an affirmation. For example, imagine yourself trading and following your trading rules. Experience yourself putting on trades in accordance with your trading methods. Mentally practice staying with the trade until your system tells you it's time to get out. Start with a profit, take a loss, and end with a profit. Mental rehearsal works wonders for the real trading.

If you violate your guidelines during a trade or trading day, redo it in your mind doing the right actions. Then you can vow to do the right thing next time, and imagine yourself trading the way your methods tell you to trade.

My Power Trading for Power Profits audio course provides a powerful way to make affirmations come to life for you. Self hypnosis tapes and CD's help you make good trading principles second nature to your trading. You are guided in rehearsing your trading so that you automatically do what you know you should do. As a trader you mentally become skilled at execution. You have decided what methods to employ and now you can facilitate those methods. You practice your skills like a top athlete mentally rehearses his flawless moves.

Trading Hesitation

When you observe a hot market or a hot stock or an unusual opportunity, you know that the volatility causes extra risk along with extra reward. Some traders become fearful or timid and sit on the sidelines until they just can't stand it any longer, and then they hurl themselves into a trade just as the savvy traders are collecting their profits.

In Kevin's Story, we watched Kevin hesitate to get out of a winning position. We watched his profits dry up and we saw him crater into a huge losing hole. Some traders never even get this far, they hesitate before they enter. Their buttons are pushed into a permanent pause. Pressing their noses against the window of the trading arena, they only window shop.

True, they don't experience monetary loss as Kevin did, but they lose opportunity and is so doing suffer a personal sense of insufficiency. Sometimes the trade we fail to take or the profit we take too soon is more painful than an actual loss. I wrote a poem—a villanelle—about one such trader.

The Conflicted Trader

The lure of winning fuels her greed.
How much she wants and wanting taunts,
But fear of losing blocks her deed.

A hesitation halts her speed.
To trade, to wait, the wanting haunts;
The lure of winning fuels her greed.

A raging market calls to feed.
Enormous wealth and now it flaunts.
But fear of losing blocks her deed.

She cannot act despite her need.
The dream of riches tied with taunts,
The lure of winning fuels her greed.

Act now, act now, her heart will plead.
It's hers to have, the movement flaunts.
But fear of losing blocks her deed.

She cannot lose! That is her creed.
Despite the hope, oh how it haunts!
The lure of winning fuels her greed.
But fear of losing blocks her deed.

Courage

"The gods cannot help those who don't seize opportunity."
—Confucius

How do we create courage where none exists? How do we change financial timidity into measured risk taking?

Courage is an emotional muscle that can be trained. Each small act of courage builds on the one that went before. Conversely, each small act of fearful inaction builds on the one that went before.

It becomes important to break the habit. You can take baby steps. Trade as small as you can, but trade. Consider trading in small increments as practice for the bigger game.

Stop looking at each trade as being all important. Group your trading into a series of trades. Take an arbitrary number, and analyze the trades once that number has been completed.

There is a theory that you cannot solve a problem from the level at which it was created. If you're asking yourself how you can keep from losing, you know you're asking the wrong question. Loss is endemic to trading. You have to give in order to receive. If you're not willing to do this, get out of the game. Spend your time in an arena in which you do find comfort.

Change your focus by changing the questions you ask yourself. Stop asking, "What if I lose?" This will never get you anything but more pain. Instead ask yourself, "What are the probabilities here?" "What if this trade is a big winner?" You can also ask helpful questions such as: "How do I protect myself from excessive loss?" "How will I protect my profits as the trade moves along?"

When we talk about courage, we're not talking about reckless abandon. We're not saying throw caution to the winds. We're talking about calculated risk and the anticipation that the risk is worth taking. Focus on the reward, and willingly balance it with the risk. Remember, winners anticipate winning. Losers anticipate losing.

> *"You have got to take risks, you have got to take chances. You have to go into life brave."*
> —**Billy Joel**

Courage overcomes fear. It's natural to have some fear when trading, after all there is danger as well as opportunity. Some fear is rational and is protective. However, when we let fear dominate, we've ruined our chances for success. That's why we need courage. Courage isn't necessary if we know no fear.

Hot Market Mistakes

While a strongly trending market bails out a lot of mistimed and misplaced trades, and causes many novice traders to think they're better than they are, it also creates temptations and chances for major mistakes.

How can you go wrong when you are given the heavenly opportunity of a really hot market? Let's look at some of the behaviors that can get you in trouble.

- **YOU CAN MISS THE TRADE COMPLETELY.**

MISSED OPPORTUNITY

> *"Opportunity passes like a cloud."*
> *"Blessings brighten as they take their flight."*
> —**Anonymous Proverbs**

It's a hot, hot market. But you stand still on the shore of this great bull market while others throw themselves into the sea. They dive easily under the waves and with strong strokes swim out beyond the breakers. Better beached than drowned you think. Huge price waves are crashing this way and that way, with two days up, one day down, two days down and five days up. The limit moves scare you. You can't get in now—you should have entered last week—even yesterday. How far will it go? Time moves. Opportunity passes like a jet. Decide now. Don't delay. So goes the patois of your indecision, your under-nerved condition. You cringe while others splash around in an ocean of money. Oh they of the cool heads riding out to sea on the crest of a big, big market. Yes. No. No. Yes. You see the surfer riding home in front of a giant wave. The surfer believes he can make it. Adrenalin pumps his will. But there you stand trembling, empty handed, empty hearted, toes barely moistened by the edge of the pounding sea. You miss the trade completely.

• YOU CAN TRADE TOO BIG.

When you get too large, you can't weather the pull backs. Margin calls and such intervene. Your nerves can't handle inevitable retracements. You jump in and out—buying the highs (you have to get back in), selling the lows (the move is over). When it's all over, your profits are negligible, or worse, you have a loss. Excessive size has a way of overriding discipline and muddying clear thought.

• YOU CAN TRADE TOO SMALL.

You may be able to stay with the trade, but when all is said and done, your results are negligible compared with your overall net worth. You failed to take full advantage of a rare opportunity.

• YOU GET OUT OF THE TRADE TOO SOON.

You rejoice in your early profit. Now it can't be taken from you. But as the market moves on in major ways, and you're not participating, you realize the seriousness of your mistake. You let a major, major opportunity elude you.

• YOU OVERSTAY YOUR WELCOME.

You've gotten so used to a market going in a certain direction, that you falsely assume that nothing will change. You continue to add to your position on pull backs, but that no longer works. Or you just leave on your position in the size it is, but you fail to protect your profits. You're oblivious to the change in the market tone and direction. Your profits shrink, or worse, you enter loss.

• YOU FIGHT THE TREND.

You short the highs thinking it has gone way too far. Only it moves higher. Either you dig in only to get out when the pain of loss is greater than the pain of being wrong, or you add to your short position as it goes higher violating the rule of never adding to a losing position. Instead, perhaps, you buy the lows of massive sell offs only to find that you've caught some very sharp falling knives. Maybe you keep adding to your position as it continues its descent. You tell yourself if you sell now, it will just turn around, but it doesn't. Your losses—and your stubbornness—grow larger.

• YOU GET IN AFTER THE MOVE IS OVER.

You wait and wait until you can't stand not being in this hottest of all markets. Then you close your eyes and hold your nose and jump in. You are too late. The move is clearly over, and you get out with another loss.

False Assumptions

There are certain beliefs or underlying convictions that can prevent you from making money in a hot market. These assumptions keep you from taking timely and right action in a hot market.

1. This move has to keep going. This is the opportunity of a life time. I'm going to make a killing.

2. This market has gone too far. It can't go any further.

3. I don't have enough money. I need more.

4. There's only so much money or opportunity in the world. Each of us deserves only so much of this limited supply. If I win big, somebody else will lose.

5. This is my only (or last) chance to make a lot of money.

6. Trading is gambling, and gambling is stupid or wrong.

7. Only the big boys win at this game.

8. I can't believe what I'm seeing. It's a set-up for patsies.

9. Other people know more than I do. The gurus are saying I'm wrong. I better believe them.

10. I've got a hot hand. I can't go wrong.

Instant Imaging

The original language of our minds is imagery. We saw before we could label what we saw. Imagery is also the language of the universe. Often we see images but are not aware of the pictures we are making because they happen so quickly. Images strengthen and make more pervasive and powerful our thoughts—for better or worse. By using images, we augment our beliefs and our emotions. Through the imagery process we can also change thoughts, emotions, beliefs, behaviors, and outward conditions.

Gerald Epstein, M.D. has developed a way to use images to "tap the power of the invisible dimension and experience extraordinary physical, emotional, and spiritual healing". People using his methods have had documented miraculous cures.

Basically, the work is done in seconds, not minutes. First, you imagine the current reality that you wish to change. If it's an illness, you picture that as best you can. If it's an emotion such as anger or fear, you make an image of that. Dr. Epstein points out that you must always first go to the pain of the disturbance before you can experience the healing.

Pain, he points out, tells us there is an imbalance. First you go to the pain of the disturbance and experience the pain of growth, and then you will be free to experience the resolution. You cannot avoid the pain because evasion only increases it. So you make a picture of the unwanted situation, and then you reverse the image to what you desire which is its opposite. For example, make a picture of your fear and then transform it into what is the opposite of your fear which might be confidence or trust or courage.

Dr. Epstein suggests you do the imaging three times a day, first thing in the morning, when you finish work, and again before you go to bed. He suggests you sit up straight in a chair with arms, your own legs and arms uncrossed. Say to yourself, "I am doing the _____ process (e.g., healing my anger process), and I take

15 seconds doing it." Keep the statement in the present tense. Close your eyes. Breathe out three times through your mouth and in through your nose. Do your visualization. Breathe out one last time, open your eyes, and leave it in the hands of the invisible realm. He suggests you do this process for 21 days and take seven days off. Often you will have your result in 21 days. If you do not, you remain nonjudgmental and continue the process.

Let me share with you an example of his work: Sit in a chair in the pharaoh position. Close your eyes. Breathe out slowly three times through your mouth, and after each exhale, inhale through your nose. Imagine yourself standing in front of yourself in a sideways profile in the posture of a question mark. Notice the expression on your face. Now observe yourself turn and face yourself and see yourself in the posture of an exclamation point. Notice the expression on your face. Breathe out and open your eyes. Do this three times a day for 21 days and take seven days off.

You can use the process of imaging to help transform your trading weaknesses. Make an image of a problem you are having in your trading. Don't avoid it. See it as it is in a simple picture. Remember you have to visualize the unwanted reality first. Now shift the image to its opposite. Stay in the present, don't go worrying about whether or not it will work. Simply be faithful to the practice for 21 days three times a day. Then take seven days off.

I try all mental exercises before I recommend them. I not only guide my trading clients through them, I do them myself as well. Earlier I mentioned my inclination to jump out of my day trades too quickly only to realize that I had chosen really quite well; and I would have had much larger profits—for the most part—waiting until the end of the day. I experience my own little hot market in individual stocks for an individual day.

I used the instant imaging exercise to cure this problem. The image that came to me, and I just let it pop up, was that of a train derailed, dead still, off the tracks at an angle. I changed this image to a set of silvery parallel tracks running straight up to heaven. My eyes traveled up the tracks, and I felt a sense of calm promise. I did this for 21 days three times a day and took seven days off. I didn't worry about whether or not it would help me. I just did it. Then I did it again for another 21 days.

"What happened?" I hear you asking. Well, I can't say I'm perfect; but I can say I'm better. And when it comes to trading, I think, better is often enough. Trading is simply not a game of perfect. It is a game of development and progress.

When you identify a major trading opportunity, when you find yourself face to face with a hot market, you can make plenty of money even if you're not perfect, even if you're simply better than you were the time before. Hopefully, you will continue to get better each time you trade. Soon you develop your own smooth style. Goodness, you still can make money if you only keep a semi-cool head in a semi-hot market. Go for it, and rejoice in your improvement as you remain open to the limitless possibilities of your trading.

COACHING PROGRAM

WANTED: TRADERS WHO ARE READY FOR BREAKTHROUGH SUCCESS!

Do you continue to make the same and similar mistakes in your trading? Do you sometimes wonder if you are your own worst enemy in the markets? Are you fed up with blocking your own profitability? Or do you simply want insurance that you can stay at the top of your game?

Only those traders who are committed to financial and individual freedom invest in themselves by hiring me as a personal self-development trading coach. Their investment rewards them exponentially.

While my coaching program does not teach entry and exit strategies, it does assist you in executing your own proven strategy. You learn how to do what you already know to do. In other words, you become as good as your methods. You begin to trade with trust, confidence, courage, and a reliable consistency.

Your psychological makeup is the major factor that makes or breaks you as a trader. I know this runs contrary to the popular belief that it's the technical system that holds the magic. In truth, learning to run your mind and your emotions is the single most important key to your trading results. Your mindset is the multiplier of your trading profits and losses.

Call me at 1-800-692-0080 to discuss whether or not this program is right for you. The openings are limited, so call now, but only call if you are prepared to make powerful changes in your life and your trading.

Audio Course

Easy Way to Better Trading Results

You know how to think about your trading, but do you really think that way?

Internalize your knowledge by using these self-hypnosis tapes. Through repeated listening you alter your unconscious associations and begin to think like a winner. You use mental rehearsal to make automatic responses based on good trading principles. You diminish the power of old fears that have been holding you back. You become optimistic about the future of your trading.

Power Trading combines conscious and unconscious learning. You learn how to consciously think as you trade and you also learn solid trading principles that operate from the powerful unconscious mind. It is a complete system for managing your mind to make money.

There are three albums of tapes: Inside Secrets of Winning Power Traders, Anatomy of Losing Trading, and Power Trading for Power Profits. You'll get my manual, Complete Guide to Trader Trouble Shooting. The first 70 who respond will also get a one hour phone consultation with me (a $300 value) and an individualized tape addressed to their special wants and needs. The cost for the full course is $477. The value is unlimited. Call me at 1-800-692-0080 today to order.

Ruth Barrons Roosevelt
165 William Street
New York, NY 10038
1-800-692-0080
fax: 212-732-3482
http://www.RuthRoosevelt.com

Partial List of Publications of Traders Press, Inc.®

7 Secrets Every Commodity Trader Needs to Know (Mound)
A Comparison of Twelve Technical Trading Systems (Lukac, Brorsen, & Irwin)
A Complete Guide to Trading Profits (Paris)
A Professional Look at S&P Day Trading (Trivette)
A Treasury of Wall Street Wisdom (Editors: Schultz & Coslow)
Beginner's Guide to Computer Assisted Trading (Alexander)
Channels and Cycles: A Tribute to J.M. Hurst (Millard)
Chart Reading for Professional Traders (Jenkins)
Commodity Spreads: Analysis, Selection and Trading Techniques (Smith)
Complete Stock Market Trading and Forecasting Course (Jenkins)
Cyclic Analysis (J.M. Hurst)
Dynamic Trading (Miner)
Essentials of Trading: It's Not WHAT You Think, It's HOW You Think (Pesavento)
Exceptional Trading: The Mind Game (Roosevelt)
Fibonacci Ratios with Pattern Recognition (Pesavento)
Futures Spread Trading: The Complete Guide (Smith)
Geometry of Markets (Gilmore)
Geometry of Stock Market Profits (Jenkins)
Harmonic Vibrations (Pesavento)
How to Trade in Stocks (Livermore & Smitten)
Hurst Cycles Course (J.M. Hurst)
Investing by the Stars (Weingarten)
Investor Skills Training: Managing Emotions and Risk in the Market (Ronin)
It's Your Option (Zelkin)
Keeping a Cool Head in a Hot Market (Roosevelt)
Magic of Moving Averages (Lowry)
Market Beaters (Collins)
Market Rap: The Odyssey of a Still-Struggling Commodity Trader (Collins)
Overcoming 7 Deadly Sins of Trading (Roosevelt)
Planetary Harmonics of Speculative Markets (Pesavento)
Point & Figure Charting (Aby)
Point & Figure Charting: Commodity and Stock Trading Techniques (Zieg)
Precision Trading with Stevenson Price and Time Targets (Stevenson)
Private Thoughts From a Trader's Diary (Pesavento & MacKay)
Profitable Patterns for Stock Trading (Pesavento)
RoadMap to the Markets (Busby)
RSI: The Complete Guide (Hayden)
Stock Patterns for Day Trading (2 volumes) (Rudd)
Technically Speaking (Wilkinson)
Technical Trading Systems for Commodities and Stocks (Patel)
The Amazing Life of Jesse Livermore: World's Greatest Stock Trader (Smitten)
The Handbook of Global Securities Operations (O'Connell & Steiniger)
The Opening Price Principle: The Best Kept Secret on Wall Street (Pesavento & MacKay)
The Professional Commodity Trader (Kroll)
The Taylor Trading Technique (Taylor)
The Trading Rule That Can Make You Rich* (Dobson)
Top Traders Under Fire (Collins)
Trading Secrets of the Inner Circle (Goodwin)
Trading S&P Futures and Options (Lloyd)
Twelve Habitudes of Highly Successful Traders (Roosevelt)
Understanding Bollinger Bands (Dobson)
Understanding Eminis: Trading to Win (Williams)
Understanding Fibonacci Numbers (Dobson)
Winning Edge 4 (Toghraie)
Winning Market Systems (Appel)

**Please contact Traders Press to receive our current catalog describing these and
many other books and gifts of interest to investors and traders.**
800-927-8222 ~ 864-298-0222 ~ fax 864-298-0221
http://www.traderspress.com ~ e-mail ~ customerservice@traderspress.com

Trader's Gift Shop

Market-related art available through

Traders Press, Inc.®

Varied selections of market-related
artwork and gifts are
available exclusively through
Traders Press, Inc.®

Currently available items are pictured on
our website at
http://www.traderspress.com and in our Traders Catalog,
which is available FREE upon request

You can contact us at:
800-927-8222 ~ 864-298-0222
Fax 864-298-0221

Traders Press, Inc.®
PO Box 6206
Greenville, SC 29606
http://www.traderspress.com

MORE OUTSTANDING BOOKS BY RUTH BARRONS ROOSEVELT

Ruth Roosevelt, author of this book has written three other outstanding books, published by Traders Press, which will help you to become a better and more profitable trader. Be sure to check them out today at **http://www.traderspress.com.**

Exceptional Trading: The Mind Game

A complete review of this book is available at
http://www.traderspress.org/reviews/revw/1470.asp

---

12 Habitudes of Highly Successful Traders

Discusses in detail 12 habitudes (habits and attitudes) that are vital to trading success and teaches you how to develop the mental and emotional skills essential to successful trading.

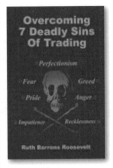

Overcoming 7 Deadly Sins of Trading

Shows you how to overcome 7 psychological and emotional barriers to trading success. Provides deep insights which enable you to develop a winning attitude and mindset.